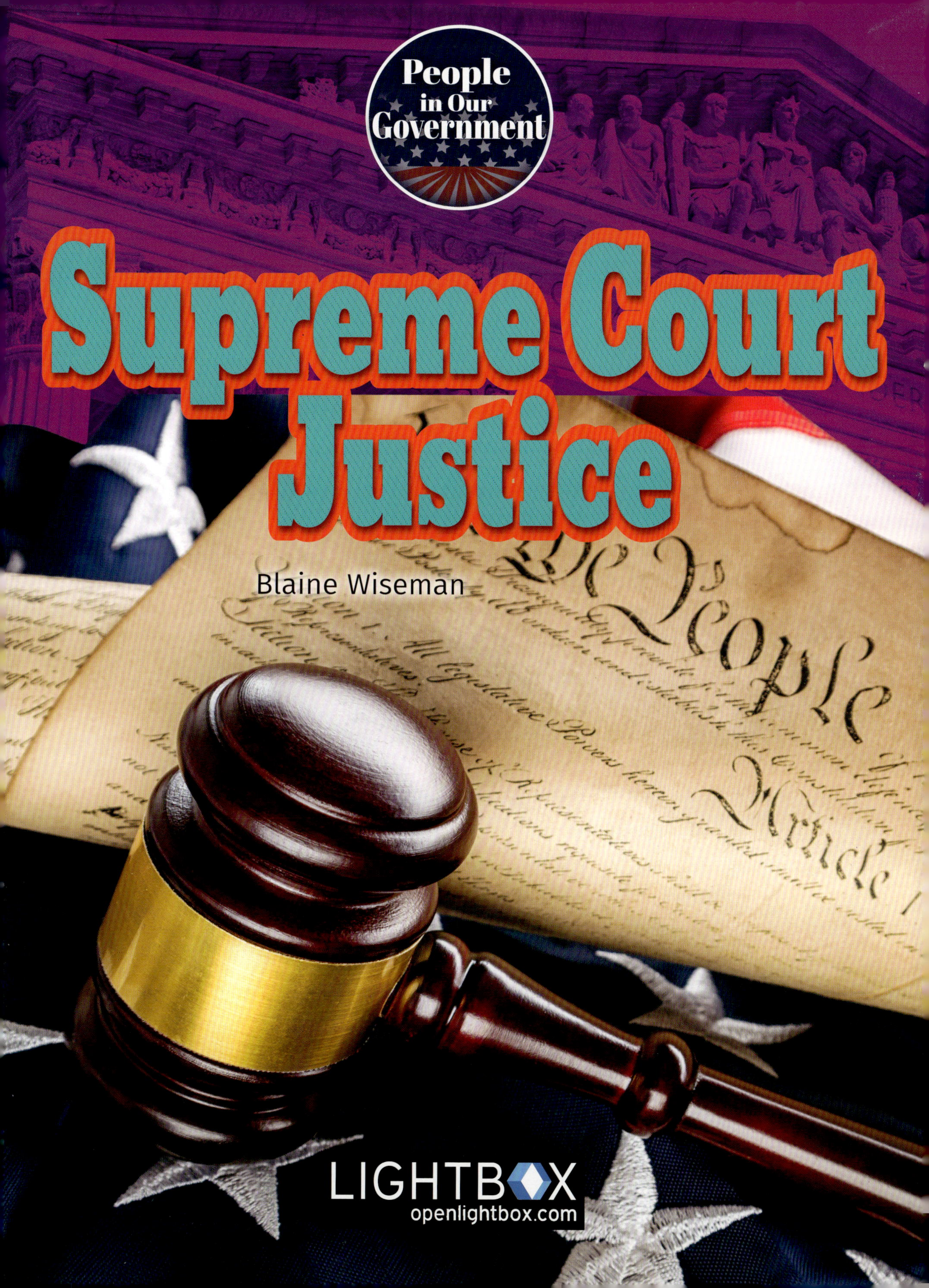

People in Our Government

Supreme Court Justice

Blaine Wiseman

LIGHTBOX
openlightbox.com

LIGHTBOX

Go to **www.openlightbox.com** and enter this book's unique code.

ACCESS CODE

LBXF3364

Lightbox is an all-inclusive digital solution for the teaching and learning of curriculum topics in an original, groundbreaking way. Lightbox is based on National Curriculum Standards.

STANDARD FEATURES OF LIGHTBOX

AUDIO High-quality narration using text-to-speech system

ACTIVITIES Printable PDFs that can be emailed and graded

SLIDESHOWS Pictorial overviews of key concepts

VIDEOS Embedded high-definition video clips

WEBLINKS Curated links to external, child-safe resources

TRANSPARENCIES Step-by-step layering of maps, diagrams, charts, and timelines

INTERACTIVE MAPS Interactive maps and aerial satellite imagery

QUIZZES Ten multiple choice questions that are automatically graded and emailed for teacher assessment

KEY WORDS Matching key concepts to their definitions

People in Our Government

Supreme Court Justice

Contents

Who Is a Supreme Court Justice?

The Supreme Court is the highest court in the United States. Nine judges **preside** over this court. They are called justices. The Supreme Court justices are the top judges in the country. The decisions they make shape the laws of the United States and impact what people, companies, and the government can or cannot do. Supreme Court justices often hold their **seat** in the court for the rest of their life.

The Supreme Court was formed by the Judiciary Act on September 24, 1789. The first **chief justice** of the Supreme Court was John Jay. He was also one of the Founding Fathers of the United States.

John Jay was the chief justice of the Supreme Court for five years.

The Government

The U.S. government is described in the Constitution. This document was written to establish the new country and its laws. The Constitution explains the three branches of government. Each branch has its own role. Together, they take care of the country and its people.

The legislative branch makes the country's laws. The executive branch carries out the laws. The judicial branch settles any problems with the country's laws.

Structure of the U.S. Government

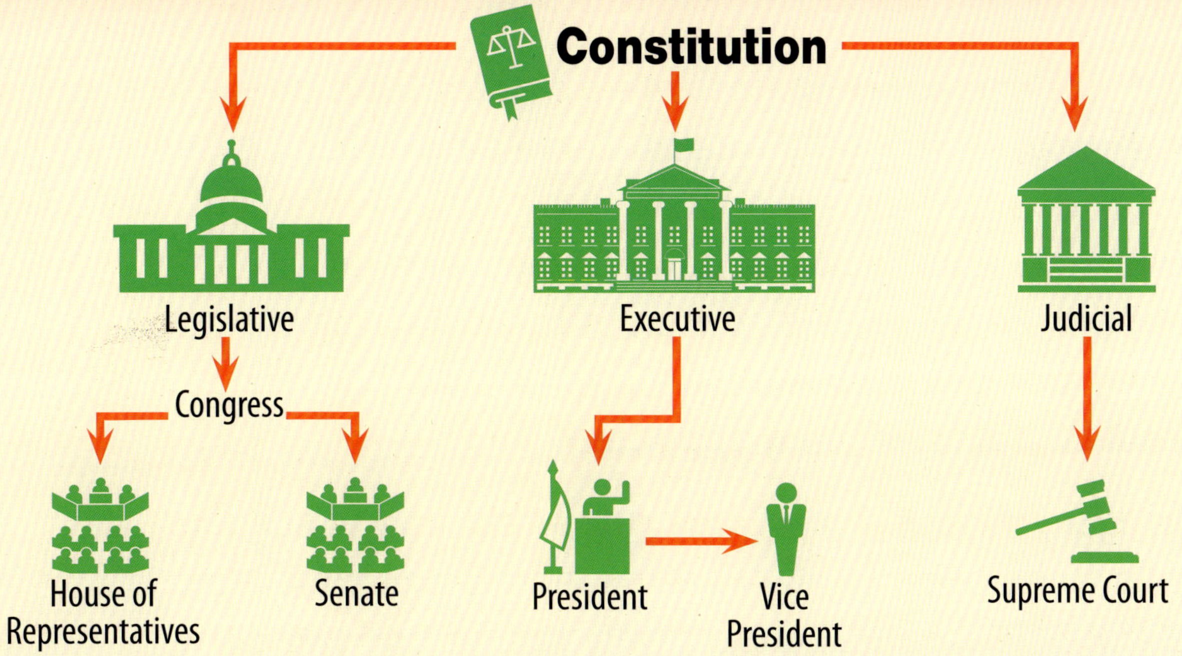

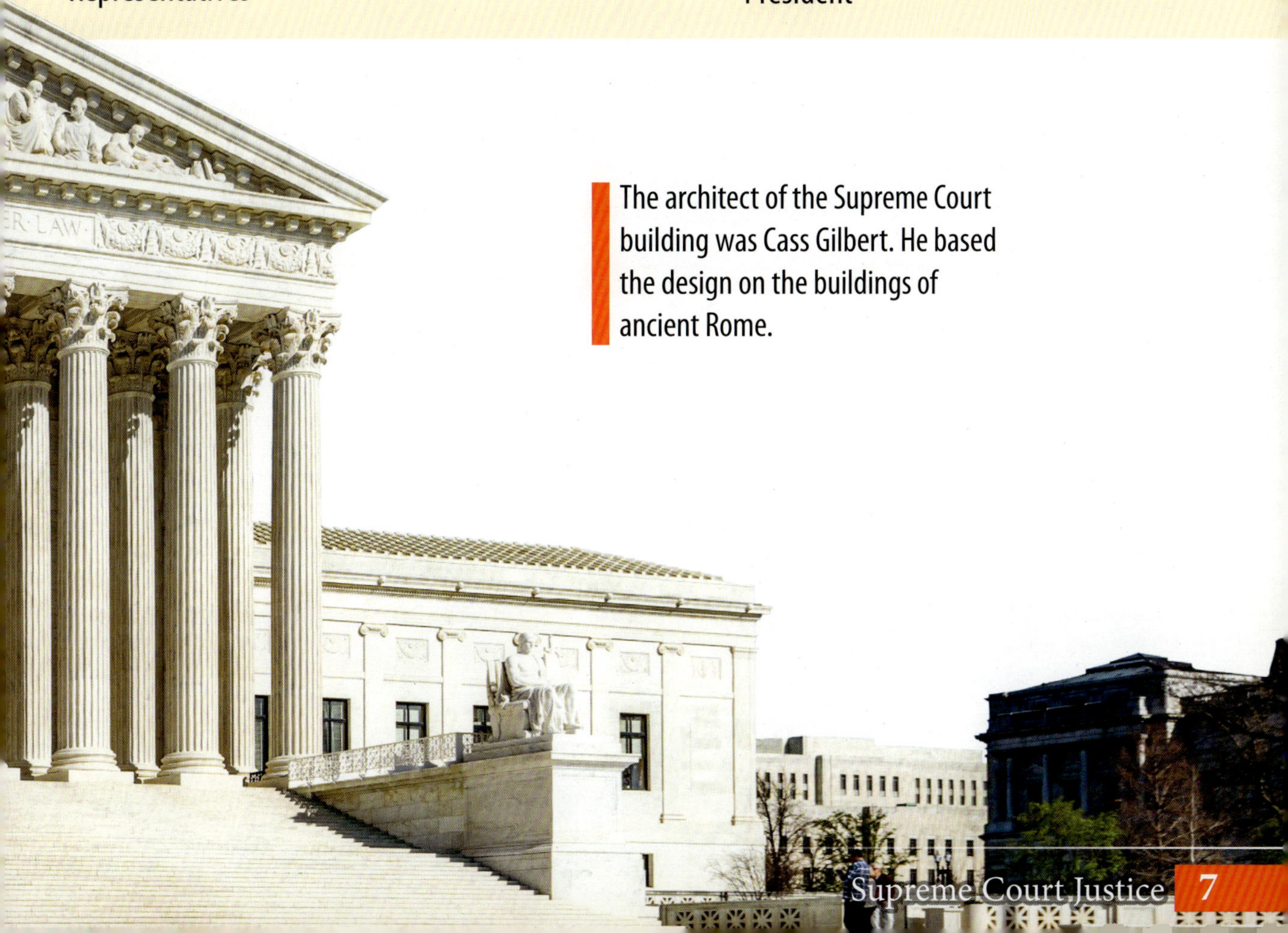

The architect of the Supreme Court building was Cass Gilbert. He based the design on the buildings of ancient Rome.

The Role

Supreme Court justices are different from other judges. They only rule on very special court cases. They do not decide if someone is guilty or innocent. Supreme Court justices decide whether a law is supported by what is written in the Constitution. The cases they rule on have been heard in **lower courts**, but have been **appealed**.

In 1954, the Supreme Court ruled that public schools had to be open to all students, no matter their **race**. Before 1954, some schools only taught one race. The Supreme Court's decision meant that students of different races must be treated equally.

Monroe Elementary School in Topeka, Kansas, was one of the schools involved in the 1954 Supreme Court ruling.

William O. Douglas was one of the Supreme Court justices who voted on the 1954 case about public schools.

There have been **114 Supreme Court justices.**

On average, Supreme Court justices **serve** for **16 years.**

The average age of a person when he or she becomes a Supreme Court justice is 53 years old.

What It Takes

The Constitution does not set any rules for becoming a Supreme Court justice. There is no minimum age that a person must be. He or she does not have to have been a lawyer or judge at a lower court first. All Supreme Court justices have studied law, though.

Thurgood Marshall was the first African American Supreme Court justice. Before he became a Supreme Court justice, Marshall was a lawyer. He argued 32 cases in the Supreme Court. Marshall was the top lawyer arguing for the 1954 fight against **segregation** in schools.

Thurgood Marshall worked with lawyers George E.C. Hayes and James M. Nabrit to win the 1954 Supreme Court case about segregation.

Getting the Job

Supreme Court justices must be **appointed** by the president. People who become Supreme Court justices often work as lawyers or judges for decades first. Their previous work experience shows what kind of justice they will be.

1 Before a justice is appointed, there must be an open seat. This means another justice has retired or died.

2 The U.S. president appoints someone to fill the vacancy.

3

The U.S. Senate **confirms** or rejects the person appointed by the president.

4

If the appointment is confirmed by the Senate, the new justice is appointed to the Supreme Court.

5

If the Senate rejects the appointment, the president must appoint someone else. The process begins again.

The Supreme Court

When the Supreme Court formed, it was located in New York City. It moved to Philadelphia in 1791. Today, the Supreme Court is located in Washington, D.C. It moved to the nation's capital in 1801. The building used today was built in 1935.

Justices' Library
The library takes up the entire third floor of the building. A team of librarians keeps the library collection organized.

The Justices' Library has more than **500,000 books**.

Two spiral staircases in the Supreme Court lead from the basement to the third floor. Each staircase features **136 steps** and **7 spirals**.

Court Chamber
This is where Supreme Court cases are heard. The nine justices sit at the front of the room behind a curved **bench**.

Justices' Chambers
Each Supreme Court justice has his or her own chamber. The chamber is his or her office space. The justice uses this room to read, think, and write his or her rulings and opinions.

Great Hall
This is the main corridor of the court building. It leads from the bronze front doors to the court chamber. The Great Hall is decorated with **busts** of every past chief justice.

Leading in Public

Justices hear cases and give their rulings during sessions called sittings. These sittings are usually open to the public. **Hearings** only happen for two hours three times a week during sittings. Justices **deliberate** and write their opinions during **recesses**.

At least six justices must be present in order for a hearing to take place.

Hearing Arguments

Supreme Court justices listen to both sides of a case during hearings. Each side has only 30 minutes to explain why the justices should vote in their favor. During hearings, the justices are also given papers with additional information that they can read during recess.

Swearing in Government Officials

Supreme Court justices are sometimes responsible for swearing in other government officials. The chief justice is almost always the person who swears in the president of the United States at the **inauguration** ceremony. Another justice usually swears in the vice president.

President Bill Clinton was sworn into office by Chief Justice William Rehnquist at the beginning of both of his terms.

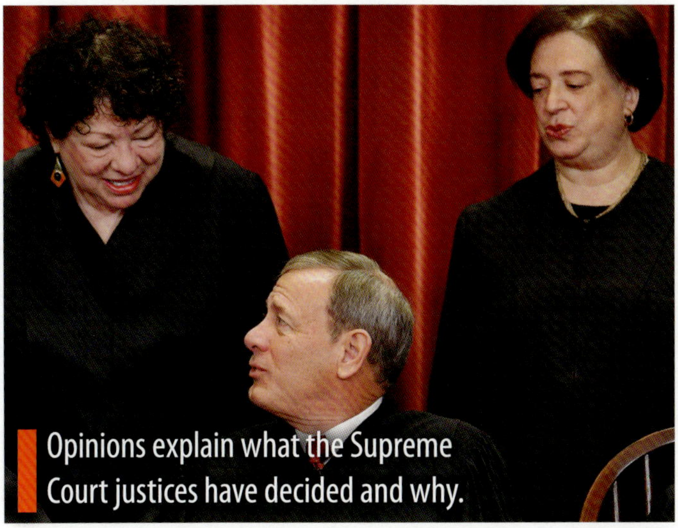

Opinions explain what the Supreme Court justices have decided and why.

Delivering Opinions and Orders

During May and June, cases are not heard. The justices sit in court to deliver their opinions and orders on each case they heard that term.

Public Speaking

Some justices make public appearances. They visit law schools to talk to students. Some also choose to teach classes about law during their summer breaks.

Justice Ruth Bader Ginsburg has written two books. She went on book tours to give talks and sign copies.

A Day in the Life

Supreme Court justices are not always in court, but they are always busy. Reading, studying, and thinking are major parts of the job. There are always more cases to review.

The chief justice has other roles outside of the Supreme Court building, such as leading impeachment trials in the Senate.

8:00 am

The Supreme Court justices arrive at the court building and go to their Justices' Chambers. They review arguments and begin writing opinions.

10:00 am

The justices enter the court for the day's sitting. The **court marshal** announces that court is in session.

12:00 pm

The sitting ends, and the justices return to their chambers. They review arguments and papers given by each side of the cases they just heard.

1:00 pm

Some of the justices go to the Justices' Reading Room to study past cases and rulings. Past rulings will help the justices form an opinion on a current case.

2:00 pm

The justices go back to their chambers to read through more case documents.

4:00 pm

The justices spend time reviewing petitions. Petitions are cases that have been sent to the Supreme Court from lower courts.

Notable Supreme Court Justices

Supreme Court justices make important decisions. The people of the United States look to the Supreme Court to explain how the Constitution affects their lives. Every Supreme Court justice has played a part in the country's history.

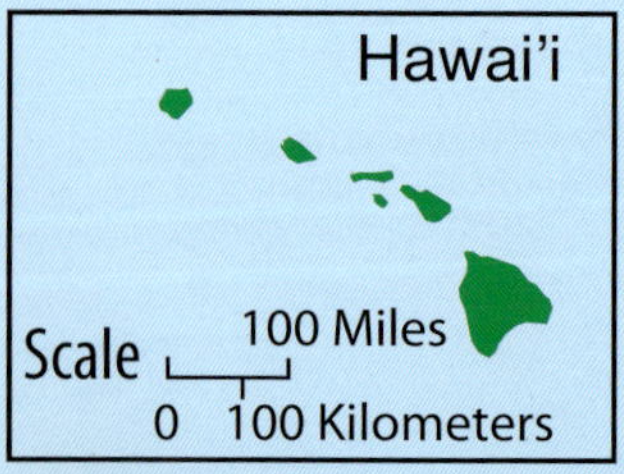

Earl Warren

Years in Office: 1953–1969

Warren was chief justice during a time of major changes in the United States. He ruled on the 1954 school segregation case. This started to change the way the country treated African Americans.

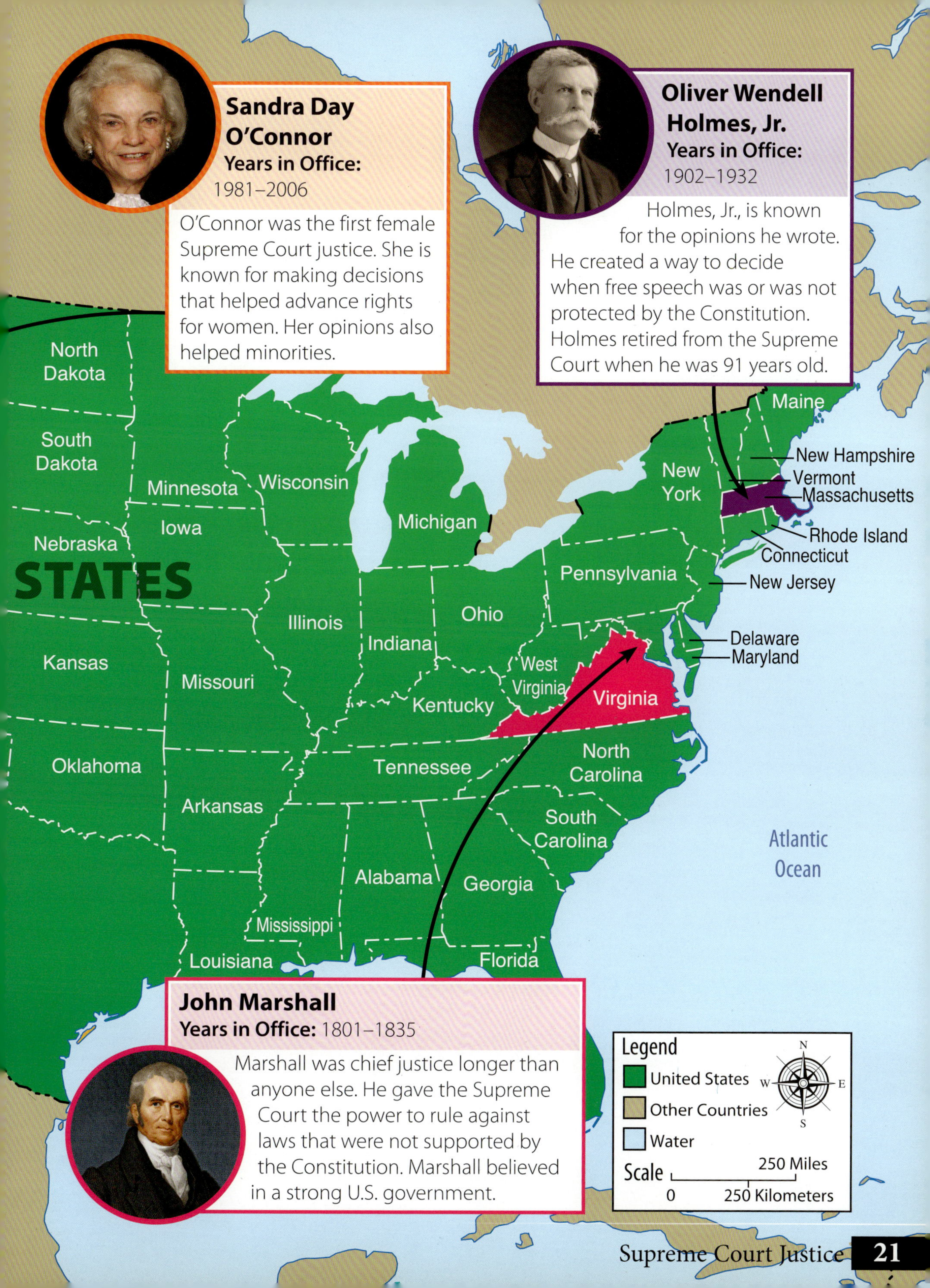

Sandra Day O'Connor

Years in Office: 1981–2006

O'Connor was the first female Supreme Court justice. She is known for making decisions that helped advance rights for women. Her opinions also helped minorities.

Oliver Wendell Holmes, Jr.

Years in Office: 1902–1932

Holmes, Jr., is known for the opinions he wrote. He created a way to decide when free speech was or was not protected by the Constitution. Holmes retired from the Supreme Court when he was 91 years old.

John Marshall

Years in Office: 1801–1835

Marshall was chief justice longer than anyone else. He gave the Supreme Court the power to rule against laws that were not supported by the Constitution. Marshall believed in a strong U.S. government.

Quiz

1 Who was the first chief justice of the Supreme Court?

2 As a lawyer, how many cases did Thurgood Marshall argue in the Supreme Court?

3 To what city did the Supreme Court move in 1791?

4 How much time does each side have to argue a case in the Supreme Court?

5 Who appoints Supreme Court justices?

6 Who was the first female Supreme Court justice?

ANSWERS

1 John Jay **2** 32 **3** Philadelphia **4** 30 minutes **5** The president of the United States **6** Sandra Day O'Connor

Key Words

appealed: asked for another hearing

appointed: assigned to a specific job

bench: the area where a judge sits

busts: sculptures of peoples' heads, shoulders, and chests

chief justice: the highest judicial officer in the United States and the head justice of the Supreme Court

confirms: makes a decision official

court marshal: a police or security officer inside a court

deliberate: to think about an issue

hearings: opportunities to present one's case in court

inauguration: a ceremony that admits someone to a government position

lower courts: courts at local, county, and state levels

preside: to be in a position of authority in a meeting

race: a large group of people who share certain physical traits

recesses: times in between Supreme Court sittings

seat: position in the court

segregation: the act of keeping one person or group separate from another person or group, such as African Americans and Caucasians

Index

LIGHTBOX

SUPPLEMENTARY RESOURCES

Click on the plus icon ⊕ found in the bottom left corner of each spread to open additional teacher resources.

- Download and print the book's quizzes and activities
- Access curriculum correlations
- Explore additional web applications that enhance the Lightbox experience

LIGHTBOX DIGITAL TITLES

Packed full of integrated media

VIDEOS

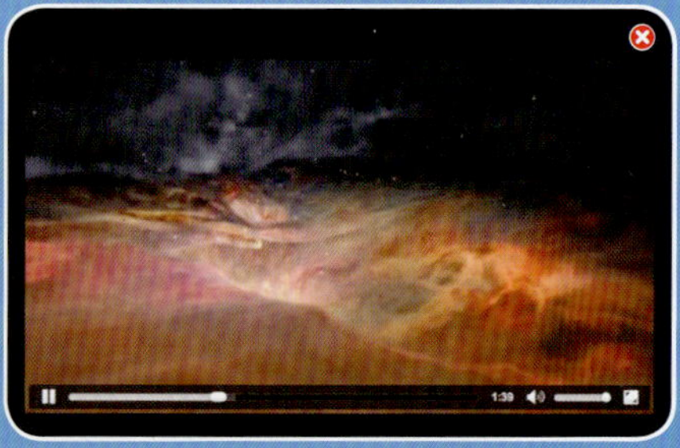

INTERACTIVE MAPS

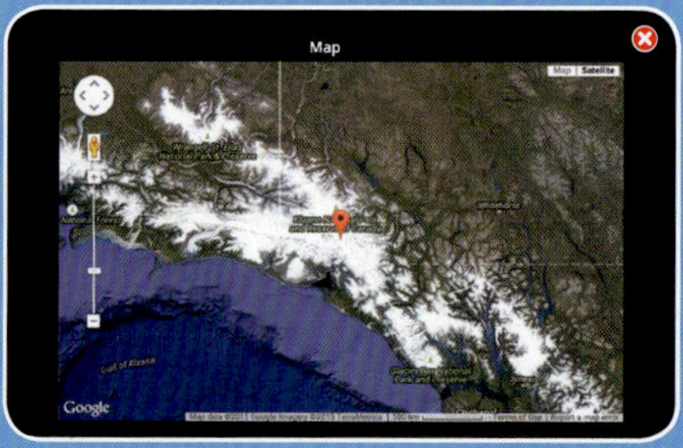

WEBLINKS

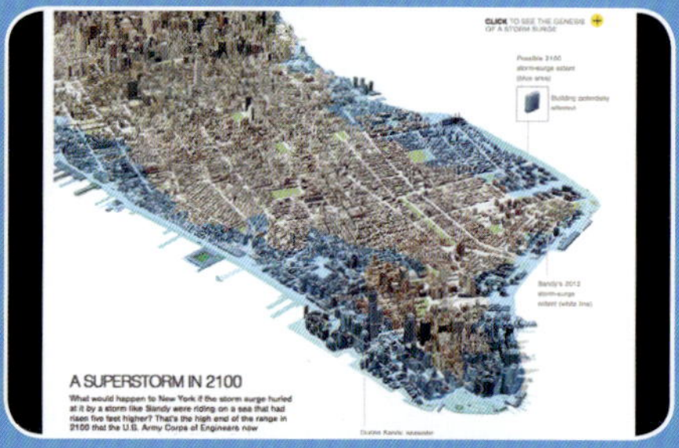

SLIDESHOWS

QUIZZES

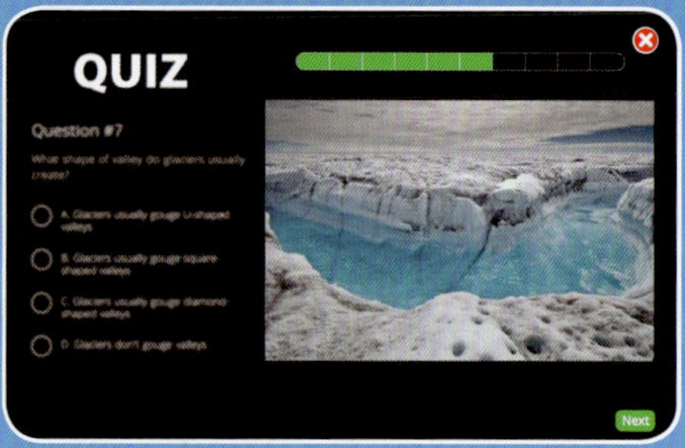

OPTIMIZED FOR

- ✓ TABLETS
- ✓ WHITEBOARDS
- ✓ COMPUTERS
- ✓ AND MUCH MORE!

Published by Smartbook Media Inc.
14 Penn Plaza 9th Floor
New York, NY 10122
Website: www.openlightbox.com

Library of Congress Control Number: 2020938417

ISBN 978-1-5105-5450-4 (hardcover)
ISBN 978-1-5105-5451-1 (multi-user eBook)

Printed in Guangzhou, China
1 2 3 4 5 6 7 8 9 0 24 23 22 21 20

062020
111019

Project Coordinator Heather Kissock
Designer Ana María Vidal

Photo Credits
Every reasonable effort has been made to trace ownership and to obtain permission to reprint copyright material. The publisher would be pleased to have any errors or omissions brought to its attention so that they may be corrected in subsequent printings. The publisher acknowledges Alamy, Getty Images, and iStock as its primary image suppliers for this title.